CRICUT MAKER

USER MANUAL FOR BEGINNERS

2020 user Guide to Master Cricut Maker, Design Space, and Projects: Tools, Set Up Procedures Advance Trick, Tips, and Troubleshooting Hacks

By

Alexander Sund

Table of Content

INTRODUCTION

Congratulations! You have one of the best craft-making machines in the world. This book is going to guide you as you learn how to use the Cricut Maker, and make awesome DIY designs with same.

The Cricut Maker is an amazing machine. However beginners, especially those who are not tech savvy have often complained of how tricky it can be to master the use of the machine.

I too had a tough time getting comfortable with the machine when I first started. I received the machine as a Christmas gift from my husband, and though I was quiet happy with the gift, I soon found out that I couldn't use it as I would have loved to. I kept seeing many cool designs on the internet and on Pintrest; and only wished I was at the very least, able to recreate them.

I knew I had to learn to use the machine by all means. See, being a stay at home mom with 2 kids, I needed a getaway…a hobby I could practice at home. I thought making DIY designs with my Cricut Maker was the perfect hobby for a person like me, so I kept researching, reading articles, blog post and even you-tube videos, while practicing with my cricut maker. With time I begin to get more comfortable using the machine and design space; making t-shirt designs, table cloths, pillows, dolls, wall decals and a whole lot of amateur designs for my home.

Along the line I introduced a friend to the cricut maker machine and guided her into mastering the device.

Now, why did I write this book?

Realizing how tasking it can be for beginners to use the cricut maker, I decided to write this comprehensive manual, detailing in a step by step manner how to use the machine and become a pro in a short time. With this book in your hands you do not have to go through the long learning curve myself and most beginners go through. In other words, this book sort of offers you a short-cut to mastering the cricut maker and creating exciting designs. All that is required of you is to follow the steps as spelt out in this manual, and by the time you are done, you will have gain some degree of mastery on the cricut maker.

The first part of the book (chapter 1- chapter 4), explains the new features in the machine and how to get simple tasks done. These tasks include finding the firmware version, finding serial numbers and how to mirror images. Within this first part of the book, you are introduced to the parts of the machine, and their functions. The accessories of the machine and their functions are explained in-depth, such that you know exactly what accessory is best for what project.

The second part of the book deals with practical projects and how to get them done. This would make a lot more sense once you have carried your first project. In this portion, techniques for projects like the print and cut and heat transfer techniques are explained. I have even lined up a few projects which you can use to get started.

All procedures are carefully explained and highlighted in simple steps. I have decided to put menu names in **bold** so that you easily follow the process pathways when skimming through this manual.

Have fun as you begin your craft making adventure with the Cricut Maker.

CHAPTER ONE

Cricut Maker machine

In August 2017, Cricut launched the Cricut Maker, adding it to their line of highly efficient cutting machines. The Cricut Maker is designed to work at faster speeds and cut thicker materials. This makes it ideal for both personal and commercial use.

The Cricut Maker allows you to use a variety of tools to work on a wide range of materials like basswood, balsa wood, fabric, leather, vinyl, felt, and paper. The Cricut Maker even allows you to cut patterns on fabrics for your projects. With accessories like embossing tips, a wavy blade, and the rotating blade, every project is made easy. You can also get more accessories depending on what project you are working on.

Unboxing the Cricut maker machine

When you buy the Cricut Maker, you get the following in the packaging. While the content may vary depending on which store or country you buy from, the following items are largely constant in every Cricut Maker box.

Each box contains the Cricut Maker machine and the following accessories;

1. Rotary Blade and its Drive Housing
2. Fine-Point Pen
3. FabricGrip™ Mat 12" x 12" for working on fabrics.
4. LightGrip™ Mat 12" x 12" for working with other materials.
5. Premium Fine-Point Blade and its Housing (this blade comes pre-installed in the B clamp).

6. A welcome book
7. The Cricut Maker Quick Start Guide
8. A USB cable
9. Power adapter
10. Materials to use for your first project.

Different parts of the Cricut maker

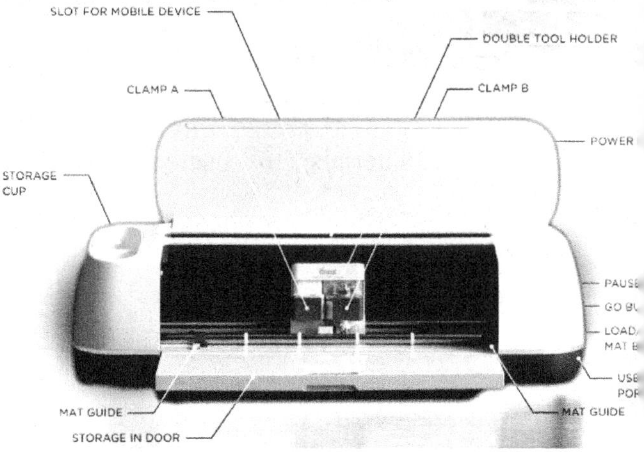

***The Tool Cup*:**

The tool cup is a product of design ingenuity. It provides a place to keep your markers, pens, pencils, and scissors while working. This lets you have an organized workspace that is tidy and uncluttered.

***Open Button*:**

This button opens up the machine to begin loading of the cutting mat and cutting operations. It is advisable to close the machine when not in use to protect it from dust and dirt. Just push the Open button and the machine unfolds like a blooming petal.

***Clamp*:**

The clamp works by keeping the blade in place so that the blades cut with high levels of accuracy. The Cricut Maker has two clamps, one for each blade housing.

***Tray*:**

The tray is where you place the cutting mat and the materials you want to cut.

***Mat Guides*:**

The Mat Guides are found on each side of the tray. The guides keep the mat in place. They roll in and out to push the cutting mat to be cut.

***Storage Compartments*:**

The storage material provides you with space to store your tools and materials as you work. It allows you to have your stuff handy and within reach.

***USB Port*:**

The USB port lets you charge up your mobile device.

***Power Port*:**

This is where the power adapter is plugged into.

***Power Button*:**

This button powers up the Cricut Maker. You also use this button to shut down the machine.

***Smart Device Slot*:**

This is an improvement on previous Cricut Devices. This slot allows you to keep your tablet or smartphone firmly in place as you work. This is especially useful if you are using Cricut Design Space on your phone or iPad.

***Load/Unload Mat/Go/Pause*:**

These are three buttons found near the Smart Set Dial. There are used to control movements of the Cutting Mat.

The Load/Unload Mat button loads the Cutting Mat with materials to be operated on by the tools. When the button is pushed and material is already loaded, it rolls out the Cutting Mat so that the material can be removed.

The Go button starts an operation. After you have loaded material to a machine, you push the Go button to commence operations.

The Pause button puts on hold any on-going operation.

Features of the Cricut Maker

***Wide Range of Materials*:**

The new Cricut Maker cuts most of the materials you will work with. It works well with a wider range of craft materials than previous cutting machines.

***Expandable Tool Sets*:**

You also have more options when it comes to the tools you can use. There are more tools at your fingertips and more effects you can create with those tools. With the Cricut Maker, you have tools such as

***Rotary Blade*:**

The rotary blade works by carrying complex movements such as gliding, and rolling as it cuts. The rotary blade cuts fast and with high precision. This blade can also cut fabrics.

***Knife Blade*:**

This blade is perfect for deep cuts. It easily cuts through stronger materials like matboard and balsa wood.

***QuickSwap Tools*:**

Another feature of the Cricut Maker is that it allows you to switch tools easily using the QuickSwap Tools feature.

***Adaptive Tool System*:**

The Cricut Maker makes use of the smart Adaptive Tool System to control the blade direction while adding up to ten times cutting power.

The Cricut Maker also comes with access to a Digital Sewing pattern library with hundreds of different patterns loaded. You also get access to patterns from established brands such as Simplicity® and Riley

Blake®. Design Space is available to Cricut Maker users and allows for Offline Mode use, and has special features like the Print Then Cut feature. Other features include the SnapMat feature. Cricut Design Space is available for iOS and Android mobile devices and tablets as well as Windows and Mac computers.

With the Cricut Maker, you can upload your designs, fonts for use at no cost and in different formats. You also have 50 ready-to-make projects and 25 digital sewing patterns you can use.

Setting up the Cricut Maker

Now that you have a good idea of what your machine is capable of, the next thing you need to do is to set it up. Where you set up your machine and how you do it determines how well you enjoy your machine. When setting up, consider placing your machine where there is adequate lighting, a power socket nearby, and ergonomics. In simple terms place your machine where you'll be comfortable working with it.

Useful tips

Always replace Pen Lids after use

When working with pens or markers, always replace the lids after use. This protects the tips of your pens from getting damaged and prevents the ink from being damaged.

Check to ensure your toolset is complete

Before packing up after a work session, ensure that all tools in a toolset are complete. It is important that before you put away a toolset in storage you ensure every blade or tip is accounted for. This helps keeps your workspace safe and prevent losses. Misplaced blades can easily cause injuries.

Keep the plastic mat covers

Your mat will come with a transparent plastic cover. You will be tempted to discard it. Don't. It helps keep the cutting mat free from dirt and dust when you use it when storing your cutting mat.

Use a Lint cleaner to remove debris

If you use your cutting mat regularly, it is easy for debris to stick to the mat. Continuous accumulation of such makes it difficult for the material to remain stuck to the mat while cutting. Rolling a lint cleaner over the mat helps rove tiny pieces of debris that make it difficult for materials to stick. This works far better than weeding out the dirt pieces individually.

Use spray cleaners to clean your cutting Mat

There are several spray cleaners available that are strong enough to remove the stubborn dirt yet mild enough not to weaken the adhesive nature of the mat. You just have to spray it and scrape off the dirt.

Use old gift cards or credit cards to scrape the mat

Old gift cards are very helpful in scraping off dirt still attached to the mat. When attaching materials to the cutting mat, bubbles may pop up, the old cards are useful in smoothening over the bubbles.

Label your cutting mat

Label your mat so that you don't load it the wrong way. Without marking which side goes in, you are going to mistakenly put it in the wrong way several times. Marking it would forestall any errors.

De-tacking your cutting mat

Upon first use of your cutting mat, you'll notice it is very sticky. It is often so sticky that it can easily damage your projects. De-tacking is the process of making your cutting mat less sticky by priming it. When you de-tack your cutting mat properly, you can easily detach projects without any damage to them whatsoever. Here is a simple way to de-tack your cutting mat.

1. Place a clean dry fabric over the cutting mat.
2. Press it firmly until it sticks.
3. Gently pull it off.
4. Repeat the process three or four times until it is significantly less sticky.

You can test if the cutting mat is well primed by placing a sheet of paper on it and then gently pulling it off. If the paper comes off without any tears, the cutting mat is well primed. If the paper tears, you will have to repeat the de-tacking process.

Making Your Cutting Mat Sticky Again

1. Use a lint roller to remove debris and pieces of dirt.
2. Clean the mat with a spray cleaner and allow it to dry.
3. Tape the edges of the mat with some painters tape so that the edges of the mat do not get sticky and stick to your Cricut Maker rollers.
4. Get a spray adhesive and spray the cutting mat.

5. Allow the cutting mat to dry overnight.
6. Prime the cutting mat if adhesive applied on the mat turns out too strong.

CHAPTER TWO

Design space installation

You will need to have a Cricut account to install Design Space. Here's how to go about it;

1. Visit **https://design.Cricut.com/**.
2. Click on "**Get Started**". It is a green box at the bottom end of the page.
3. A form will appear on the next page. Fill in your details and create a password.
4. Read the terms and conditions of use and tick the "I accept the Cricut Terms of Use" box.
5. If you want extra content such as tutorials, deals, and the latest information, you can accept them to be sent to your email address.
6. After these, you can then select the "Create User ID" button.

7. When a user account has been created, a confirmation page will appear.
8. Further questions may be asked in a form that will appear, answer the questions accurately.
9. The option to download the Design Space software will appear. Select "**Download**".
10. A window will pop up after the installation is complete guiding you through the process,
11. Read and accept the terms of the agreement.
12. The software will be installed.

Getting Cricut Design Space uninstalled

To uninstall Cricut Design Space, you follow these steps

1. Go to **Control Panel** on your computer
2. Go to **Programs**
3. Select **"Uninstall Program"**
4. A list of programs will appear, select **Cricut Design Space** and select **Uninstall**.

Finding your machine serial number

The serial number of your machine is usually under your machine. It is printed on a label and stuck beneath the machine. The serial number is usually 12 digits and contains both numbers and alphabets. All Cricut Makers have a serial number that begins with the alphabet Q.

Difference between the Cricut Maker and the Cricut Explore Air

Both machines can take in materials that are up to 12 inches in width. The Cricut explore air, however, is limited to about 100 different material types. The Cricut Maker, however, can cut about 300 different types of materials. The Cricut Maker can work with 12 different tool types for cutting, writing, scoring & other pro-level effects while the Cricut Explore Air can use just 4 tools and these tools can only score, cut and write.

The Cricut maker surpasses the Cricut Explore Air in that it is a commercial-grade cutting machine. Both machines grant users access to a free design app for iOS, Android™ Windows®, and Mac. Both Machines are Bluetooth enabled. You can also connect them to other devices through a provided USB port.

Subscribing to Cricut Access

Cricut Access is a paid service that allows Cricut users to have access to fonts, designs, images, and ready-to-cut projects. Membership of Cricut Access comes in three categories.

The perfect starter plan

This plan works well when you are sure if you want to commit long term. It starts at $9.99per month.

Annual Plan

With this plan, you pay for a year's access to the service. When you do the math you'd see that you pay $7.99 per month – instead of $9.99. The annual charge is $95.88.

Premium Plan

This plan gives you all the benefits of the other plans. With the premium plan, you get huge discounts on fonts, images, and ready-to-cut projects. You also get free economy shopping when you buy stuff amounting to over $50. The premium plans start at $$119.88.

Using the Cricut Maker Bluetooth with

Connecting the Cricut Maker to your Mac via Bluetooth (For Bluetooth Enabled Macs)

1. Keep your Cricut Maker close to your Mac.
2. Open **the Apple Menu** and select **System Preferences**.
3. Select the Bluetooth icon, ensure Bluetooth is switched on.

4. Select your Cricut Maker machine from a list of available Bluetooth devices.
5. Select **Pair**
6. Use the code 0000 to pair.

Connecting the Cricut Maker to your Android device via Bluetooth

1. Keep your Cricut Maker close to your android device.
2. In the **Settings** menu on your mobile device, select **Bluetooth**.
3. Switch on Bluetooth.
4. Select Cricut Maker from the available Bluetooth devices.
5. Pair both devices
6. Your machine will now be able to cut from your android device.

Connecting the Cricut Maker to your Windows PC via Bluetooth (for Bluetooth Enabled PC)

1. Keep your Cricut Maker close to your personal computer.
2. Launch the **Start Menu**.
3. Click on **Settings**.
4. Select the **Devices** option.
5. Switch on the Bluetooth function.
6. Select **Add Bluetooth or Other Device**
7. Choose Bluetooth, if the Cricut Maker is on, it will appear on a list of Bluetooth devices available.
8. Use 0000 as pairing code if you are prompted for one.
9. Click Connect to pair.

CHAPTER THREE

Basic Cricut Maker Tools

These are the essential tools you will need for simple projects. There are several other tools that you can use for specialized tasks that can be purchased subsequently. Here is a collection of essential tools you will need to get started on your craft making journey.

Knife Blade & Housing

This blade is particularly useful for cutting wood and materials that are up to 2mm thick. They are excellent for projects involving wood and similarly hard materials. This blade wears out after a few times of use. There are replacement blades you can buy which work fine.

Scoring Stylus

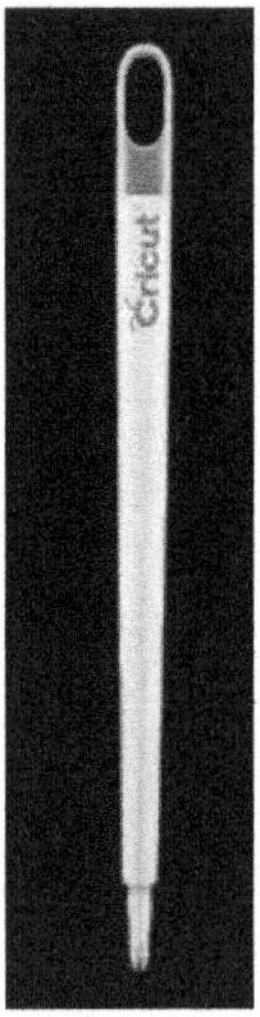

The scoring stylus helps you make accurate fold lines and creases on your material.

Rotary Blade

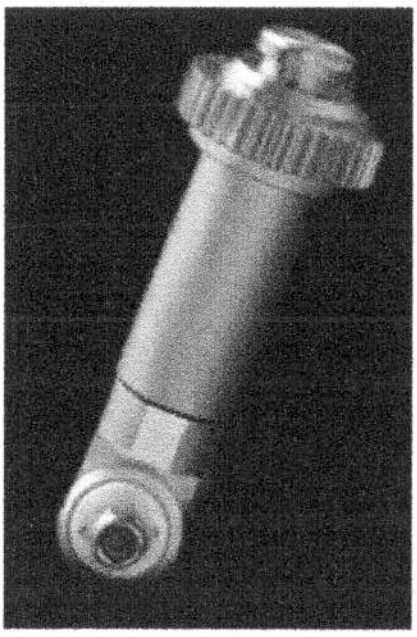

This is a special blade that works excellently with fabrics.

Premium Fine Point Blade

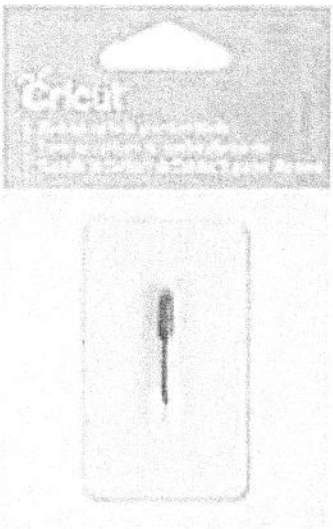

This blade comes in the Fine Point Blade housing already installed in your machine. It works well with Vinyl and paper materials, cutting them easily without any issues. Unlike the knife blade, the fine point blade does not easily wear out and is long-lasting.

Scraper and Spatula

The scraper and the spatula help you take off materials from the cutting mat.

Weeding Tool

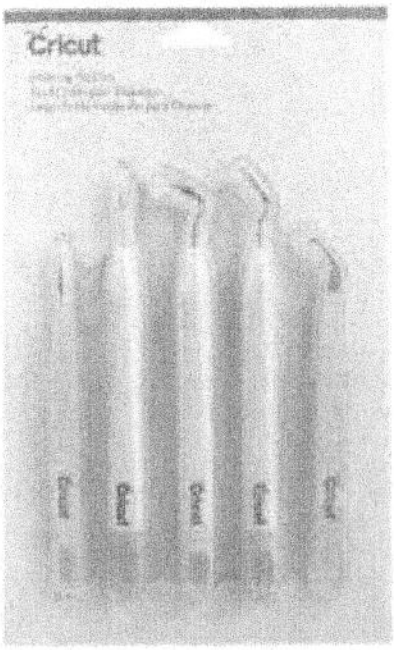

This tool helps you take off pieces of cut materials that are stuck on the cutting mat. The tool sometimes comes in a complete tool kit.

Selecting Pens to Use

The Cricut Maker allows you to use pens to write and draw simultaneously. The pens are non-toxic and are permanent once they get dry. The pens differ in tip size and create different effects. The type of pen you select should depend on what effect you want to create.

- There are calligraphy tip pens with tips ranging from 0.2 to 2.0 in size. You can check the Black Set, it a good calligraphy pen set.
- The Metallic Pen Set is also another pen set. They work well on card

stock paper. You have a variety of colors with the metallic pen set.

- There is the Classic Pen set which gives off a regular pen effect.
- The Glitter Bright Set gives the glitter effect.

Finding the current firmware version of your Cricut Maker

You can find out the firmware version of your Cricut Maker using these steps.

1. Switch on your Cricut Maker and connect it to your computer.
2. Login to your Cricut Design Space account.
3. Click on the Account menu (☰). It is on the top left corner of the screen.
4. Select **Update Firmware**.

5. A list of machines will drop down. Select Cricut Maker from the list.
6. The computer will detect your machine. If your firmware is up to date, you will be notified. If it is not, you will be asked to update it. The latest Cricut Maker firmware version, for now, is 4.175.

Note: You can only use a computer (Mac or Windows) to check the firmware version of your Cricut Maker. You cannot use the apps (iOS or Android) to check it.

Finding the current Design Space Version

For Windows Computers

1. Select the arrow on the taskbar to open hidden icons.

2. Allow your mouse pointer to hover over the Design Space icon.

3. The plugin version will appear.

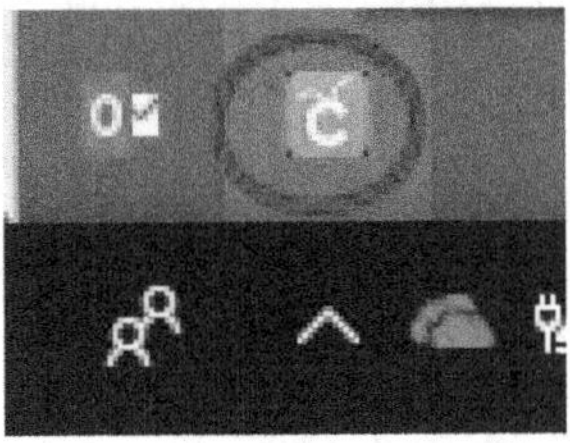

Checking Design Space Version for Mac

1. Click on the Cricut icon. It is found at the top right end of the screen.

2. Click on "**About**."

3. A small window pops up showing information that includes the current version.

For iOS Devices

1. Launch the Cricut Design Space App and log in.

2. Open the app menu. It is in the upper left corner of the screen (it usually shows your details like initials and profile picture).

3. The version number of your Design Space app will be found at the bottom of the menu.

For Android Devices

1. Launch the Cricut Design Space App and log in.

2. Tap on the app menu on the top-lcft of the screen.

3. The version number of your Design Space app will be written at the bottom of the menu.

How to use Fast Mode

The Fast Mode is a feature limited to **Cricut Explore Air 2** and **Cricut Maker** machines. This feature allows you to cut and write at speeds that are up to two times the normal cutting and writing speeds. You can use the fast mode on Cardstock materials, Vinyl, and Iron-on materials.

Here's how you turn on Fast Mode on your mobile device and computer

- When you are about to write or cut the material, move to the Cut screen.

- Having selected the materials to be cut in the previous screen, the Fast Mode option will appear.
- Turn on the Fast Mode option

The image below illustrate the process.

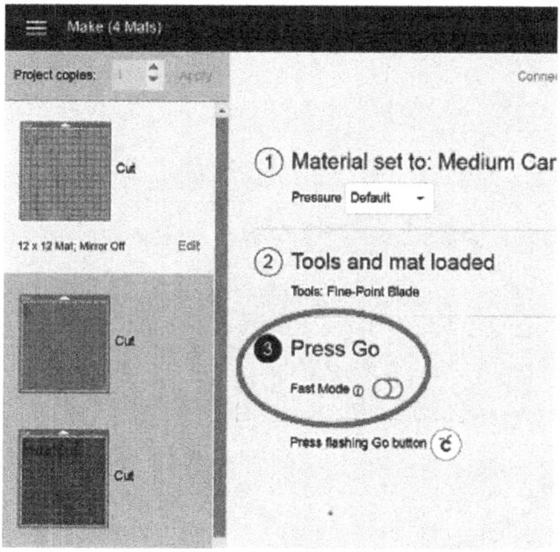

Note: It is normal for your Cricut Maker to make noise that is louder than usual when cutting or writing in Fast Mode.

Choosing a Material setting

The Cricut Maker has pre-set settings that guarantee the best results on defined materials. With the Smart Set Dial, you do not have any business with speed, or pressure settings all you do is to turn the dial to the right material and push the Go button.

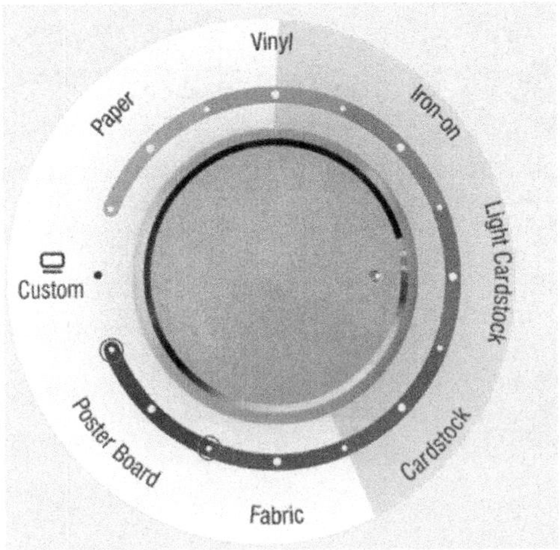

There are pre-loaded settings for materials like Paper, Vinyl, Iron-on, Light Cardstock, Cardstock, Fabric, and Poster Board. After working on Design Space and making your settings there, you simply turn the dial to the material you wish to work with. For instance, you wish to cut Vinyl, after making all the settings on Design Space, you turn the dial on the Smart Set Dial to Vinyl before you push **Go** to begin cutting.

Custom Cut Settings

Your Cricut Maker cuts more than just seven types of materials. To give more flexibility, there are several other materials settings you can access via Design Space. This gives you more precise cutting settings. Here is how to use Custom Cut settings.

1. Launch Design Space and sign in.
2. You can create or open an existing project.

3. Your Cricut Maker must be turned on and connected to your computer.

4. Proceed to the Project Preview screen.

5. Turn the smart set Dial to **Custom**

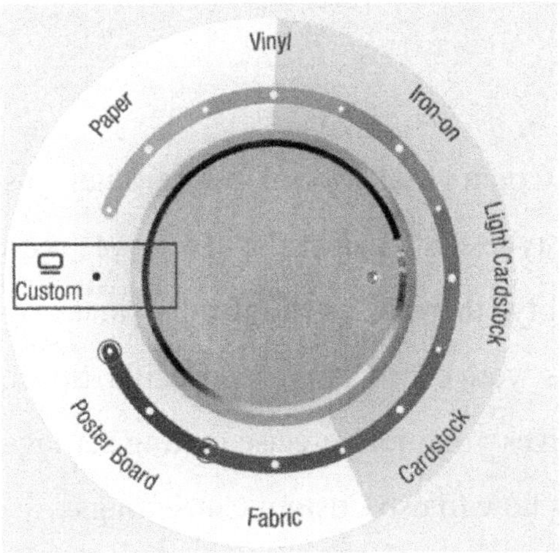

6. Click on **Browse All Materials.**

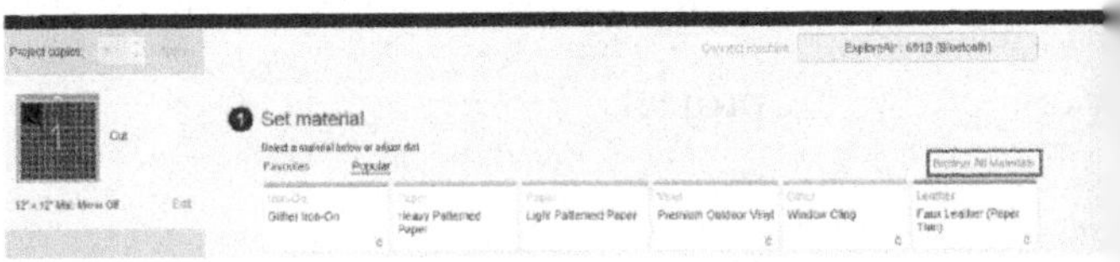

7. A drop-down list will appear with the names of materials. Select the material you wish to work with.

Creating Custom Settings

Sometimes the custom settings available may not come close enough to the material you want to cut. You can, however, create your custom material that can be as close as possible to the material you wish to cut. Here is how it is done.

1. Go to Menu (☰)
2. Select **Manage Custom Materials**, or select **Material Settings.**

3. Scroll down to the bottom of the page and click on **Add New Material**.

4. Create a name for your new material and click **Save**.

5. With the new material saved, you can adjust the following parameters for cutting the material:
    - Cut Pressure- This is the pressure with which the machine cuts the material. You can use the sliders to adjust this.
    - Multi-cut – This makes the machine cut over the same object several times. It works well with thick materials.
    - Blade Type

6. Click **Save** to save your new material.

7. The new material will now be available in the list of materials.

Editing Custom materials

To edit or delete a custom material you have created;

1. Launch the Menu (☰)
2. Select **Manage Custom Materials**.
3. Select the material
4. Click the Edit button
5. Edit as appropriate or Click on Delete.

Removing and Replacing Accessory Adapters

Here is how to replace accessory adapters safely.

1. Open the accessory Clamp A.
2. Put your thumb under the accessory adapter and put pressure from under while you push down from the top

with your other fingers. The adapter will come out of the clamp.

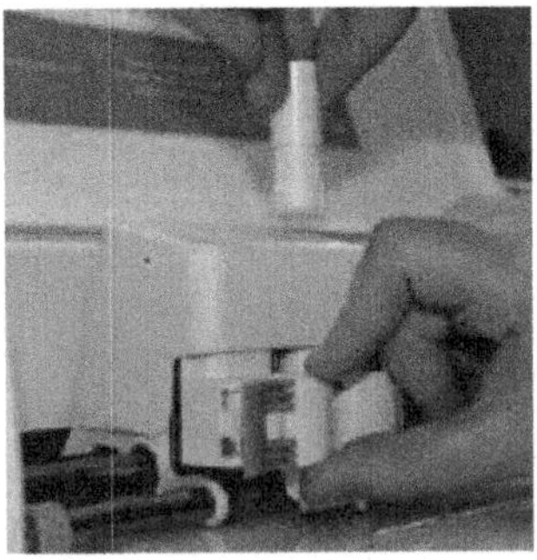

3. To put back an accessory adapter, place your finger under the clamp to steady it and put it in the adapter from the top.

4. Apply gentle pressure until the adapter snaps into place.

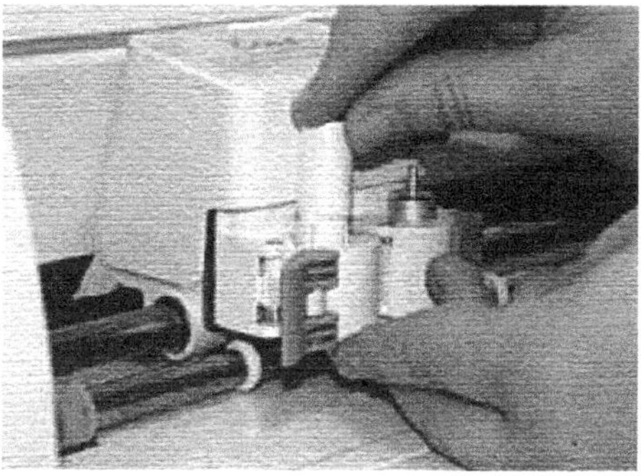

Cricut Maker Project Ideas

There are several amazing things you can do with your Cricut Maker. Are you having a hard time with project ideas? Here are a few to get you started.

1. Vinyl Decals and Stickers
2. Sewing Patterns
3. Homemade Cards
4. Christmas tree ornaments

5. Jigsaw Puzzles
6. T-Shirt transfers
7. Baby Clothes
8. Felt Toys
9. Wedding Invitations
10. Fabric Keyrings
11. Halloween Decorations
12. Iron-on Vinyl work
13. Cake Toppers
14. Gift Tags
15. Pin Cushions

A few of these projects will be further explained subsequently in this book.

CHAPTER FOUR

How to run Test Cuts

Test Cuts would indicate if your settings are okay to be deployed. Test Cuts usually prevent damage on the main material, since any wrong setting would be detected and corrected. Here is how to run test cuts.

1. Prepare any simple design of your choice on Design Space. The design should be small and simple.
2. Place the design on the edge of the workspace, so that it will be cut on the edge of the material.
3. Send the design to be cut by your Cricut Machine.
4. Load the material and press "**Go**" on your cutting machine. The machine will cut it.
5. After it is cut, unload the machine and check the material. If it doesn't

meet your specifications, you can adjust the settings and try another cut.

Using Cartridge Adapters

Unlike previous machines, the Cricut Maker does not have a slot for a physical cartridge. However, if you have cartridges you can still get them linked using the Cartridge Adapter. Here is how to do it;

1. Plug the cartridge adapter into the USB port of the computer.
2. Sign in to your Cricut Design Space account, select the option "**Link Cartridges**" from the menu.
3. Click on "Adapter" from the list of options.
4. Plug the Cartridge into the adapter when Cricut Design Space prompts you.
5. Cricut Design Space will detect the cartridge, once the cartridge is detected, click "**Link Cartridge**".

How to install free fonts on Cricut Design space

If you can't find your favorite fonts on Cricut Design Space, or you wish to use free fonts from third party sites, follow these steps below;

1. Visit the site where you wish to get thee fonts and download the font.
2. If the font was downloaded in a zipped folder, extract the font.
3. Install the font by double-clicking on it.
4. Once installed, your font will appear on Design Space. If it doesn't appear in Design Space, refresh the Cricut Design Space.

How to Mirror Images when cutting HTV

When cutting materials that will be transferred using heat, the material is usually placed on the cutting mat face down. If the image is cut into the material that way, the images will appear backward. Hence it is necessary to cut the materials mirrored so that when the image is transferred, it comes out the right way.

How to Mirror on Windows and Mac Computers

1. After working on your design, select "**Make It**". This will take you to the Project Preview page.
2. Select a mat and then turn the **Mirror** option on to flip the design. Always turn the Mirror option on when working on designs that would be ironed on.

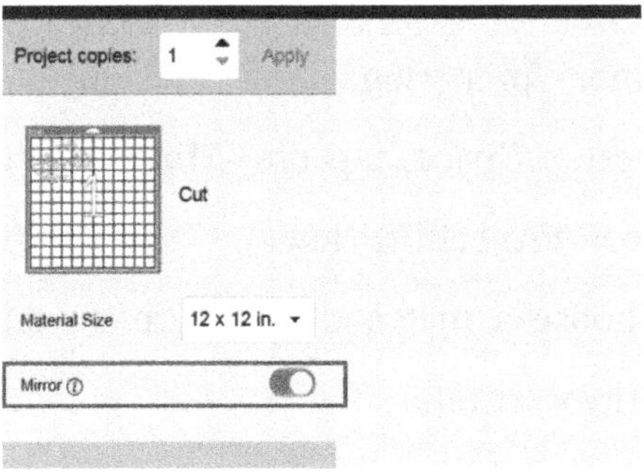

3. Click on "**Continue**" to complete cutting.
4. Usually, if you select any iron-on material without turning on the

mirror feature, Design Space will remind you to turn it on before cutting begins.

5. In this case, go to "**Edit**" (it is usually next to the mat), turn the **Mirror** function on.
6. Click on "**Done**".

How to Mirror on Android and iOS Devices

1. After preparing your design on Design Space, tap on "**Make It**" to go to Project Preview.
2. Choose a mat and then turn on the Mirror feature.

3. Select the image on the top left corner to dismiss the list of mats. Click on "**Continue**"

4. The software will remind you to mirror the images if you forget to.
5. You can Mirror each mat by tapping each mat and turning the mirror function on using the edit function.

6. Cricut is now ready to cut

How to change blades of the Cricut Maker

1. Open the second Clamp B and gently remove blade housing.

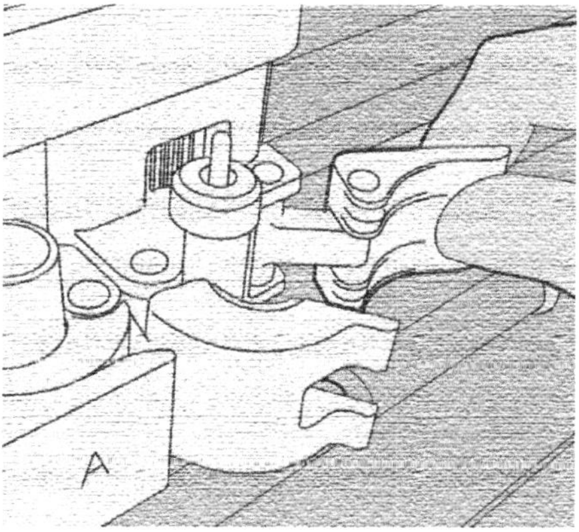

2. Place the blade housing in Clamp B. Ensure the hosing is resting on the top of the clamp. For Rotary and Knife blades, the gears have to fit together.

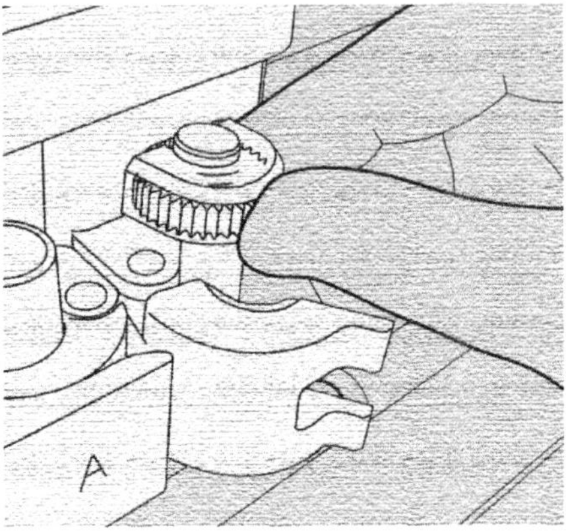

3. You can then close the clamp.

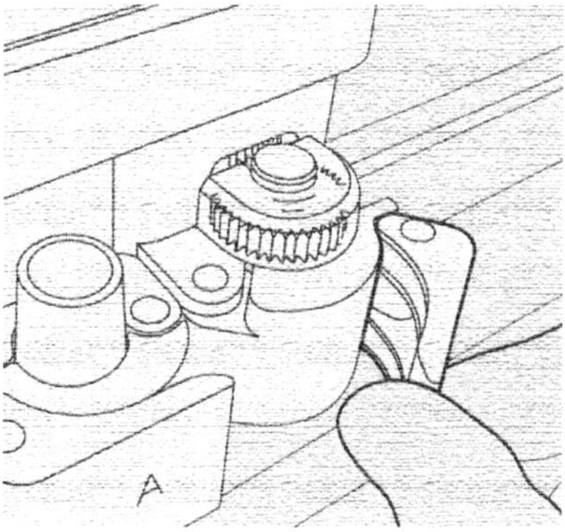

CHAPTER FIVE

Using Print and Cut in Cricut Design Space

The Print and Cut feature in Cricut Design Space is a wonderful feature that is sometimes underrated. To use the feature, a printer and the Cricut maker are used in conjunction to create amazing designs in single and multiple layers. It is one of those features that everyone can use and is not limited to any level of expertise. You will learn everything you need to learn about this feature in Cricut Design Space with your Cricut maker to print your designs.

What is Print and Cut?

The Print and Cut feature is an awesome feature that allows you to create designs with an image or text in Cricut Design Space. You can use colors to easily create professional designs and have them printed on your printer. Your Cricut maker then cuts out the design.

Projects that can be made with the Print and Cut feature

There are so many projects that you can use the Print and Cut feature to make. The list is endless. Among them are;

- Gift tags

- Invitation cards
- Stickers
- Calendars
- Banners
- Bookmarks, etc.

Types of images that can be printed

The Print and Cut feature can pretty use any image type by conversion. The types of images that can be printed include;

- JPG
- PNG
- SVG

You can also upload your image file and font and have them print and Cut.

How to use Print and Cut

You can use this feature to create designs with an image or text. We shall explain how to create designs with an uploaded image first. Follow these steps to use Print and Cut feature.

1. Log in to your Design Space account.
2. Select the Green Box in the top right corner and select **New Project**.
3. Select "**Upload Image**". Let's use a jpg file for example. The upload button is on the left side of the screen.

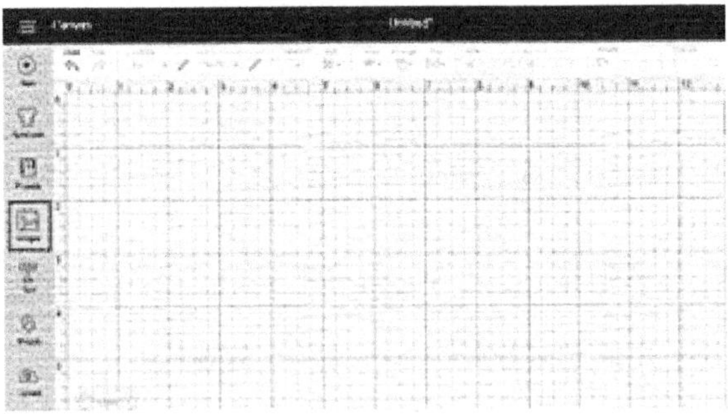

4. Browse through the files on your computer and select your desired image.

5. Select **Open**.

6. Select your image type and click continue (most people choose complex as they image type).

7. You will be taken to the **Select and Erase** screen. This where your Cricut maker would be able to cut.

8. Select the areas that you want to erase around the image with your mouse. After you are done, select **Continue**.

9. The next screen will show you your new file. If you would want to make any adjustments, you can always go back and make corrections. Once you have certified your file as okay, save image as **Print then Cut**.

10. Click the **Save** button in the bottom right part of the screen.

11. Click on the **Insert** image button in the lower right corner and select your saved image. Insert it into the canvas area.

12. Resize your image. The standard measurement for print then cut shouldn't be more than 9.25 x 6.75. Remember that you won't see print then cut while resizing. Cut will appear as the Line type while the Print will be denoted as Fill.

13. Once you are done resizing, click on **Make It**.

14. Your image will be ready to be print then cut. Load your print then cut the image onto your mat and click Continue in the bottom right of the screen.

15. Connect your Cricut Maker and select **Send to Printer**. Select the type of printer you want to use and print.

16. A dialog box will open, which will allow you to find your printer and select the number of copies that you need.

17. Click print. Your image will be printed to your home printer. Select your material for print.

18. That's not all. Load your mat into your Cricut maker.

19. Press **Go**.

20. Your maker will start cutting your designs. Remove design from the machine when you are done.

21. Cut out excess material from your design for fine finishing.

22. You have completed your project with the Print and Cut feature.

Alternatively, you can use the Print and Cut feature with Cricut Design Space images if you don't have an image to upload. Cricut Design Space has a catalog of custom images, including Print then Cut images that you can use to cut on your Cricut Maker. Print the Cut images or Printable images that don't need to be converted.

The process is practically the same, except that you won't be uploading pictures. Follow these steps to use the Print and Cut feature on your Design Space and Print then Cut images.

1. Log into your Design Space account.

2. Click on **New Project** by selecting the + symbol in **My Project**.

3. In the left toolbar, click on **Images**.

4. Browse through the large library of images for your suitable image. If you want to opt for Printable images, you can find them in the filter section. Select your image and click **Insert Images**.

5. Click on the insert image button in the lower right corner to load an image into the canvas area and select your saved image.

6. Resize your image. The standard measurement for print then cut shouldn't be more than 9.25 x 6.75 and less than 8.5 x 11. Remember that you won't see print then cut while resizing. Cut will appear as the Line type while the Print will be denoted as Fill.

7. Once you are done resizing, click on **Make It**.

8. Your image will be ready to be print then cut. Load your print then cut the image onto your mat and click Continue in the bottom right of the screen.

9. Connect your Cricut Maker and select **Send to Printer**. Select the type of printer you want to use and print.

10. A Printer dialog box will pop up, which will allow you to find your printer and select the number of copies that you need. Always keep the bleed on to eliminate any white borders on your designs.

11. Click print. Your image will be printed to your home printer. Select your material for print.

12. That's not all. Load your mat into your Cricut maker.

13. Press the flashing "**C**".

14. Your maker will start cutting your designs. The sensor on your machine will read all the black lines. Remove from the machine when you are done.

15. Cut out excess material from your design for fine finishing.

16. You have successfully used the Print and Cut feature.

Now that we know how to use the Print and Cut feature to create designs, let's show you how to use the Print and Cut feature with text.

Follow the steps below to know how to do this;

1. Open your Design Space.

2. Select the Green Box in the top right corner of the screen and click on **New Project**.

3. In the left toolbar, click on **Text**.

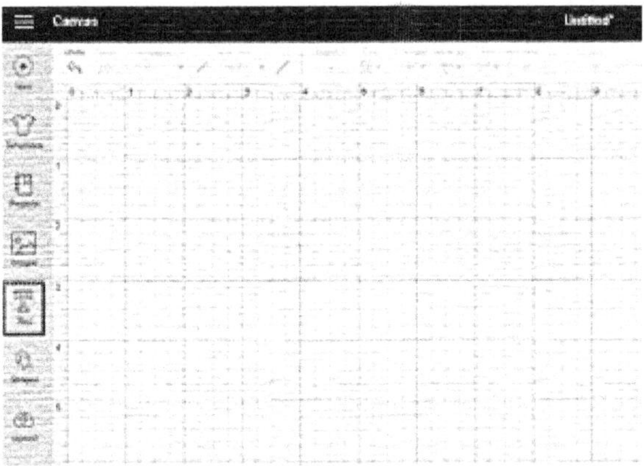

4. Write any text you want in the text box. After that, use the toolbar to adjust the letter spacing, fonts, etc.

5. Now if your text is on a single layer, you have to change the Fill to **Print**. If you are using multiple layers,

repeat the same process you did for the single layer. Alternatively, you can use the Flatten tool to turn the layers into print at once.

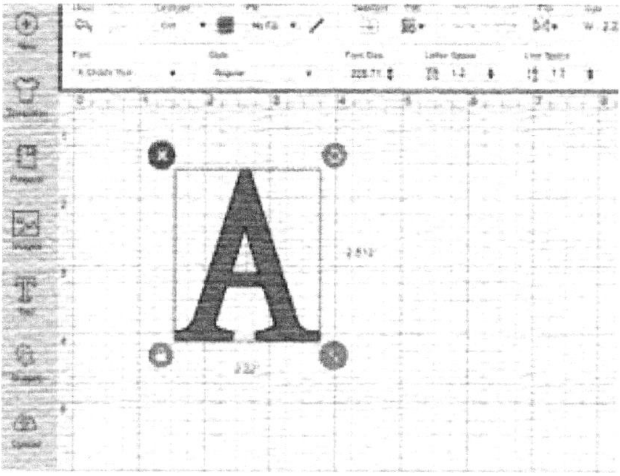

6. Click **Make It** in the top right corner of the screen.

7. The Mat Screen will pop up. Click on **Continue**.

8. Connect your Cricut Maker and select **Send to Printer**. Select the

type of printer you want to use and print.

9. A Printer dialog box will pop up, which will allow you to find your printer and select the number of copies that you need. Always keep the bleed on to eliminate any white borders on your designs.

10. Click **Print**. Your image will be printed to your home printer. Select your material for print.

11. That's not all. Load your mat into your Cricut maker.

12. Press the flashing "**C**".

13. Your maker will start cutting your designs. The sensor on your machine will read all the black lines. Remove

from the machine when you are done.

14. Cutout excess material from your design for fine finishing.

15. Congratulations! You have successfully used the Print and Cut feature with text.

Note that before you use your Cricut Maker machine, you would have to calibrate it. Without calibration, your machine would have difficulties in using the right blade. You can also use colored materials with the Cricut Maker machine because it has an advanced sensor.

Materials that can be used

The material that can be used for Print and Cut depends on the type of printer you are using. If you are using printers like inkjet, HP Envy 4500, Epson Sure Color P400, and the Canon Pixma, you won't have any issue with your printer ruining the material you are printing on.

However, most printers work on the following materials:

- Printable Vinyl
- Cardstock
- Burlap
- Chipboard
- Paper
- Sticker paper
- Vellum
- Printable Iron-on Vinyl, etc.

Uploading your image to Design Space

Cricut Design Space supports DIY designs, which means that you can design and upload a picture or an image that is unavailable in the image library. You can either use Adobe Illustrator or Photoshop to create your designs.

There are two types of images you can upload; basic images and vector images. Cricut Design Space supports both file types. The methods of uploading them are different, but the result is the same. Basic images such as JPG and PNG are uploaded as a single layer, while vector images like SVG are separated into layers. It is the same process you use for uploading a vector file and a basic file.

To upload an image;

1. Open the Cricut Design Space environment and click, **Upload Image** from the left-hand menu.
2. Browse through the list of uploaded files and select the image.
3. Select, **Insert Image**.
4. Select from the type of images Cricut Design Space will ask you.
5. Another tab will open, select the part of the image you want to cut and the one you don't want to.
6. Select whether your image is a regular image or a print-then-cut image.
7. The file will appear in your work area on the screen. Sometimes, the imported files don't come at the correct dimensions, so you would

have to edit. The “edit” menu is on the right of the screen.

8. Select, **Go** in the top right of the screen and cut your design.

Adding Fonts

Cricut Design Space simplifies the process of adding that special touch to your project using fonts. Adding fonts is easy and you can either use the custom or system fonts or use your fonts.

The following steps will explain in details how to use a font in a Cricut Design Space:

1. In the work area of your Cricut Design Space, click the **Text** icon to start writing your text.
2. Add your text. Ensure the text is highlighted.

3. Click on **Font**.

4. From the drop-down on the taskbar, select **System Fonts**. All your fonts in the system will load at once. This may take some seconds.

5. Select your preferred font.

6. The selected or highlighted text will be displayed in your new font.

7. That's it. Your text is now in your new font.

You can also use the Cricut pen to write fonts. This works by changing the Line type of your text from "Cut" to "Write". These pens are easy to use to write and are similar to handwritten texts. Just make sure that before you start writing, you must have selected the font to use.

The Contour Feature in Cricut Design Space

The Contour feature is a tool that enables you to hide a portion of an image layer. It does this by eliminating any unwanted cut lines. Using the contour tool is easy and will show you in the steps below.

1. Select the image to be contoured and click **Ungroup** at the upper right corner of the Layers panel.

2. Select the layer you want to contour by clicking **Contour** in the layers panel.

3. A hide contour window will pop up. You will see some cut lines on the image. Select the cut line you wish to hide. The hidden contour will change to a light shade, indicating the lines will no longer show.

4. Once you are finished hiding the line(s), exit the contour window.

If you made a mistake and you wish for your hidden contour to be restored, you can click on the hidden lines and they will be restored on the canvas.

Linking up Script Letters

When using script fonts, you must link up the script letters. This is one big mistake that most people make and one step they often miss. You will learn the process of linking your Script Letters in the following steps.

1. Type your word in the text box of your canvas.

2. Select your desired font.

3. Click on the Text box and select **Ungroup to Letters**.

4. Drag the letters next to each other with your mouse. Don't overlap unnecessarily and make sure the line of letters is as natural as possible.

5. Highlight the letters and weld. Doing this will make sure that no letter is cut out.

6. If some letters disappeared, it could be that you overlapped the letters. Start the process again and make sure you correct the spacing. You can increase the size to avoid any overlapping mistakes.

7. You have successfully linked up script letters.

Spacing of Letters

Leaving a lot of spaces between lines or letters is a common mistake that most people indulge in. However, the error can be fixed in some simple steps that will be written below.

1. Type the word you want.

2. Click the text box and select **Ungroup to letters**.

3. The letters will be moved to the appropriate places individually. Watch out for any extra space and correct it when you observe it.

4. Attach the letters. Else, they won't stay together.

CHAPTER SIX

Vinyl Tricks

The Cricut Maker machine can do so much more for you and that includes making things better for you while you are crafting. If you are a beginner, you will certainly enjoy some amazing vinyl tricks in this chapter like how to easily cut vinyl for decorations and clothing.

Cricut Transfer Tape

The Cricut Transfer Tape is designed to make the transfer of vinyl designs to project materials or surfaces easy. It makes it easy for you to position your design in the right place.

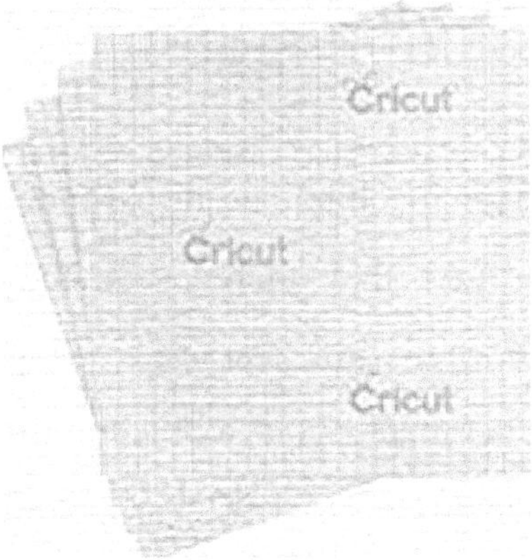

Cricut transfer tape

Cricut transfer tape

There are different types of transfer tape that you can use. There is the paper transfer tape, strong grip transfer tape, and regular transfer tape.

Paper transfer tape is typically made of paper. It’s mostly used for curved projects. However, this transfer tape is not something you can reuse.

Strong grip transfer tape is stronger and more sticky than the paper and is used on thick vinyl.

The regular transfer tape is commonly used and is suitable for all pieces of vinyl. An example of this type of regular transfer tape is Oracle MT80P.

Using the Cricut Transfer Tape

1. Place the vinyl clear liner down into your Cricut Maker mat.
2. Select and size the image(s).
3. Load the mat into the Cricut Maker machine. Adjust the setting of your machine by selecting "**Browse all materials**".

4. Select the type of vinyl you are using, so that the liner is intact. This is called a kiss cut.

5. Tap the **Go** button.

6. Weed any piece away from your images using weeding tools that are found in the Weeding Tool Set to make the process neater and faster.

7. Take your transfer tape. Put it over the top of your project, rubbing it from one to the other till it's completely placed on the vinyl. This is to avoid any wrinkles or bubbles beneath the transfer tape. Remember to place the adhesive upside down.

8. Grab a roller to smoothen the transfer tape over the vinyl. This is to get bubbles or wrinkles out should they

exist and make sure that the vinyl stays glued to the transfer tape.

9. Peel the vinyl away from the liner. This should be done at a 45-degree angle. If the vinyl refuses to come off the liner, use your roller to rub the tape onto the vinyl till it comes off the liner.

10. Once you are done, then, it's time to put the vinyl on your project.

11. Place the vinyl over your project material in the place where you want it.

12. Grab your roller once again to rub the vinyl on the material till you are sure it's tight.

13. Carefully pull off the transfer tape.

14. You are done using your transfer tape.

Types of Vinyl to layer

There are two major types of vinyl layers.

- The adhesive vinyl
- The heat transfer vinyl

The Adhesive Vinyl

The adhesive vinyl type ranges based on thickness, brand, colors and different sizes. You can apply the adhesive vinyl on your design and then, do some weeding. After that, you apply the transfer tape. Transfer the vinyl to your design material and remove it after use.

Other brands of adhesive vinyl types include:

Oracle 631, Oracle 641, Oracle 651, Oracle 751, Oracle 951, Oracle 5600, Oracle 6510, Oracle 8300, Oracle 8510, Oracle 8710, Oramask, Oraguard, Glitter StyleTech FX,

Glitter StyleTech Ultra, Siser Removable EasyPSV, StyleTech 4000, Siser Permanent EasyPSV, and so many others. Most of this adhesive vinyl has up to 2-year durability and comes in several colors.

While these adhesive pieces of vinyl are good to use, some are more suitable for outdoor use than indoor use. For example, the Glitter StyleTech FX is more suited for outdoor use.

The Heat Transfer Vinyl

Heat Transfer Vinyl or HTV as it's widely called is not a sticky vinyl like the adhesive. Instead, it makes use of heat before it could be applied to fabrics. The shiny part is placed face down, while the back of the vinyl faces upwards using the mirror technique. Once you are done with weeding, you can now paste it on your material. There is no transfer tape required because it is not sticky.

Like the adhesive vinyl, the HTV comes in a variety of colors and brands. Among them are:

Siser EasyWeed, Siser EasyWeed Electric, Siser Glow, Siser Holographic, Siser Brick 600, Siser StripFlock Pro, Siser Metal, Siser VideoFlex Glitter, and so many others.

Setting up a surface for layering

Before you try to use an adhesive, you have to make sure the surface you are using for the layering is suitable. Most pieces of vinyl work on solid surfaces like wood, plastic, and glass. There is every chance that dusts will accumulate on the surface, so apply some alcohol on it and wipe down and across the surface.

Vinyl on Wall

You can personalize your wall with some vinyl wall décor made with your Cricut Maker machine using a Cricut cartridge. That is another pretty amazing thing you can use your Cricut Maker machine for. The steps for making vinyl wall decorations will be explained later in this chapter.

If you don't know the processes involved in applying it to your wall, follow these simple steps.

1. Select the perfect space for your decal or image design.

2. Clean the surface where you want to apply your decal by removing dirt and oil with a sponge and soap.

3. Place the decal on the wall. Remove the adhesive side and paste it on the selected area slowly.

4. Use a roller to remove any bubble or squeeze.

5. Remove the paper backing that is protecting the face of your decal or image design.

Iron-On Vinyl

Iron-on vinyl is a type of Vinyl material that works with the application of heat. It's a heat-sensitive material that can be used on fabrics, wood, paper, metals, etc.

There are three methods that you can use to apply iron-on vinyl on your material – a heat press, an iron, and an EasyPress are what you can use to adhere to your material.

Weeding Iron-On Vinyl

Iron-on vinyl is one of those materials that are convenient to work with on a Cricut Maker machine. It can work on difficult surfaces like wood and makes it easier to layer your projects. You can simply cut your design, weed it, and then, iron it on.

As stated here, after you just have cut your design, you have to weed it. Weeding iron-on vinyl is removing unwanted materials from your project. It's a simple process, but you need to be careful while doing it, especially if your design is a little complex.

Before you start weeding, make sure you mirror your design. Cricut will send you a warning, reminding you to do this, since you are using iron-on vinyl material. If you don't mirror your image, the weeding will turn out pretty bad because you are meant to cut the back of your vinyl. Hence, there is need to mirror the images.

Once your image has been cut, weeding is the next process. It can be indeed frustrating if you have bad eyesight, but it’s pretty easy if you follow the steps below to learn how to weed your design.

1. Find a weeding hook that is convenient for you. Cricut offers a variety of weeding tools with several weeding hooks.

2. Keep your material on your Cricut mat. It’s very convenient because it

will keep your project steady and make it easier to weed your vinyl.

3. If you have some difficulties seeing your weeding lines, use the Cricut BrightPad. It's a small thin light of that emits light. You can place your vinyl on top of it and use the light to weed.

4. The Cricut BrightPad may not be enough, so make sure you weed under a bright light.

5. Start from the top and weed down and across. Weed slowly and carefully and ensure that nothing is removed from the back of the material.

6. Check if you missed weeding any piece, once you are done.

Applying Iron-On Vinyl

Before you decide to apply iron-on vinyl, you need to cut it first. Follow the steps below to cut your Cricut iron-on vinyl.

1. Log into your Design Space.
2. Click on the **Images** tab on the left side of the panel and select an image from the huge library.
3. After you have selected your image, they will appear in the canvas area.
4. Click on the **Edit Toolbar** to resize appropriately to fit your project material.
5. You can change the color of your image by clicking the **ColorSync Panel** in the upper layers panel on the left. Drag and drop the object into the layer of your desired color.

6. Select **Make It**. A screen will pop up with a preview of your image.
7. Since you are using iron-on vinyl, you must mirror it. We have discussed the importance of mirroring an image in this book. When you click **Mirror** in the sidebar, your image will flip backwards on the mat.
8. Click **Continue** and proceed to connect your computer to your Cricut Maker machine.
9. Select your iron-on material from the list of materials.
10. Flip your iron-on vinyl material back on your mat. Insert the mat into the Cricut machine and press the arrow button on it to hold your mat.

11. Press the **Go** button and your Cricut maker will cut out your project.
12. Press the arrow button again to release your mat.

After you are done cutting, the next thing is to weed it. We have shown you the tutorial on how to weed your iron-on vinyl.

Once you are done weeding, applying the vinyl on your material is next. Remember, you can use the Cricut EasyPress, normal iron, and a heat press to apply the iron-on vinyl on your material. We shall teach you how to use the whole three methods to adhere to your iron-on vinyl on your material.

How to use Adhesive iron-on vinyl on your material With Cricut EasyPress

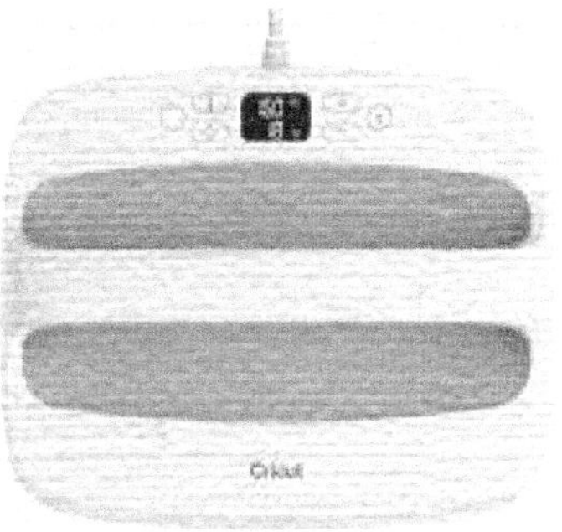

Cricut EasyPress

Any size of EasyPress could be used to apply an iron-on vinyl on your material. Just make sure that you are using the one you are most comfortable with.

Before you transfer your design image to your material, you have to do a pre-press with your EasyPress for about 5 seconds.

The aim is to flatten the material so that it can be ready for the design to be added.

You can decide to iron with your EasyPress directly on a plastic or anywhere that seems more convenient. Follow the process below.

1. Press down with your EasyPress on the design image with steady pressure. Don't forget to put a plastic carrier sheet between your EasyPress and your vinyl.

2. Press for some seconds and return to base to cool a bit.

3. Peel the back of the plastic carrier sheet if the vinyl sticks. If it doesn’t, put the plastic back and press for some seconds again.

4. Remember to press the design image on your material front and back, with 10 – 15 seconds interval.

5. You have successfully used the EasyPress to apply your design image to your material.

How to use adhesive iron-on vinyl on your material with a heat press

The process of using the heat press is similar to that of EasyPress. Follow the steps below to use a heat press.

1. Set your heat press to 315° and 15 seconds.

2. Do a pre-press with your heat press for about 5 seconds. The aim is to flatten the material so that it can be ready for the design to be added.

3. Add your design image, press down with your heat-press, and lock it. Wait for the countdown to elapse. Ensure you place Teflon pressing sheets between your heat press and your design image.

4. Allow the heat press to cool a bit before peeling off the Teflon sheet. If your design image doesn't stick, put the Teflon sheet back and press down again.

5. Flip the material on its back and press down for 10 – 15 seconds.

6. Once you're done, remove the Teflon sheet.

7. Congratulations! You have successfully used the heat press to adhere to your design to your material.

How to use adhere iron-on vinyl on your material with an iron

Adhering your image on material is simple with an iron. The process is also similar to the other two sources of heat.

1. Set your heat press to 315° and 15 seconds.

2. Do a pre-press with your heat press for about 5 seconds. The aim is to flatten the material so that it can be

ready for the design to be added. Do this before the iron heats up.

3. Place a plastic material on your design image before pressing down. You can also place a cotton fabric on top of the plastic material if you feel the iron will melt the plastic material when it's unevenly hot.

4. Press for 15 – 20 seconds. Make sure you press around the image if it's larger than your iron. However, don't move the iron around. Turn your material around instead and let your iron press down from a fixed position.

5. Allow the heat press to cool a bit before peeling off the plastic sheet. If your design image doesn't stick, put

the plastic sheet back and press down again.

6. Flip the material and press down on its back for 10 – 15 seconds.
7. Once you are done, remove the plastic sheet.
8. Congratulations! You have successfully used the heat press to adhere to your design to your material.

This is all there is to know about vinyl. Ensure you follow all the steps in this tutorial carefully.

CHAPTER SEVEN

Other Sample Projects

Cricut Maker can make other sample projects like snowflakes, Halloween spiders, and other wonderful designs, using the Design Space.

Snowflakes

You can make cool snowflake designs with your Cricut Maker machine and enjoy have some fun with it in snowflake parties. A snowflake party is incomplete without some snowflake decorations.

Snowflake spiral decorations can be made with something from Cricut that's called party foil. You can create snowflake spirals with it with your Cricut Design Space. You will need to cut it, weed it, and apply iron-on vinyl. It follows the same procedure as making iron-on vinyl decorations.

Halloween Spiders

Halloween party is one of those themed parties that everyone loves to attend. Several costumes and designs like the Halloween spiders are everywhere. Do you know that you can use the Cricut Maker to make some of these pretty designs and costumes including the Halloween spiders?

Creating Halloween spiders is simple if you have the materials and are using the right Cricut blade. You can use the rotary blade and fine point blade to create Halloween spider costumes and designs for your party.

What you need to create the Halloween spider design are:

- Your Cricut Maker
- Any Cricut Felt
- Rotary Blade
- Hot Glue Gun
- Mat

Follow the process below. We will be creating two spider web images in two red and white.

1. Log into your Design Space account.
2. Click on **New Project** by selecting the + symbol in **My Project**.
3. In the left toolbar, click on **Images**.
4. Upload your spider images. Select the images and click **Insert Images**.
5. The images will load into the canvas area.

6. Once you have your file in your Halloween spider file in your canvas, click the **Make It** button.

7. It will take you the mat preview. If you created two spider images, select 2 project copies.

8. Tap **Apply** and select **Continue**.

9. Choose your Cricut Maker machine from the list on your screen.

10. Select **Felt** from the list of materials.

11. Select **Edit Tools** to choose your rotary blade.

12. Cut out your felt with the rotary blade. Once you are done, use the Cricut Maker to cut felt.

13. Your spider images will be on the mat. Use a scraper to eliminate straps off the mat.

14. You may be left with small pieces of your spider images, you can use glue to attach and decorate them to your perfection.

15. You have just made spider designs. You can take it and have fun with it at your Halloween Spiders party.

Herringbone Themed Wall Anchors

Do you know that DIY Herringbone Themed Wall Anchors can help make your home a little tidy? A piece of wood mounted on the wall can hold up some properties and free up your small space. Unsurprisingly, it's one of those things that the Cricut Maker machine can make.

It's not so difficult to create a herringbone themed wall anchor. All you need is a pine board, a wall hook, finish paint, some drills, and of course, your Cricut Maker machine.

1. Paint the wooden board with whatever color you desire.

2. Let it dry for about 24 hours.

3. Click on the images tab on the left side of the panel and select an image from the huge library. There is also the Herringbone pattern available, so you can decide to use it.

4. After you have selected your Herringbone pattern, they will appear in the canvas area.

5. Click on the **Edit Toolbar** to resize appropriately to fit your project material. If you are using a

rectangular piece of wood, make sure the size of the image is a rectangle.

6. Select **Make It**. A screen will pop up with a preview of your image.
7. Click **Continue** and proceed to connect your computer to your Cricut Maker machine.
8. Select your iron-on material from the list of materials.
9. Insert the mat into the Cricut machine and press the arrow button on it to hold your mat.
10. Press the **Go** button and your Cricut maker will cut out your project.
11. Press the arrow button again to release your mat.
12. Weed out excess material.

13. Apply the vinyl to your pine board.
14. Use the drill for holes and attach your hooks.
15. Place your anchors and hang it on the wall.

You have successfully made a herringbone themed wall anchor.

Halloween Bat

Making a Halloween Bat is pretty simple with the Cricut Maker. All you need is your Cricut Maker, Cricut Felt, rotary blade, hot glue gun (optional), and a mat. Just like for the Halloween spider.

To make a Halloween Bat, follow the same processes used in making the Halloween Spiders. You just have to replace the spider with the bat.

Iron-On Vinyl Metal Design

You can make cute designs with your Cricut Maker machine, using the iron-on vinyl heat transfer on a surface metal. Amazing right? So, it's not only fabrics or paper projects you can use an iron-on vinyl on.

The process of using an iron-on vinyl on metal to create a design is the same as using an iron-on vinyl on fabrics. The difference is you use the metal, in place of the fabric. You cut out the design with your Cricut Maker machine, weed, and then, use an iron, heat press, or the Cricut EasyPress to iron the design on the metal. However, you have to be cautious of the heat because the metal can get hurt easily. The process of cutting, wedding, and applying an iron-on vinyl using an iron, heat press, and the Cricut EasyPress has been explained in Chapter 6 of this book.

HTV on Wood Front Porch Design

Do you know that you can use Heat Transfer Vinyl or HTV on wood to make front porch designs? In this tutorial, you will learn how to make a front porch design on wood using HTV.

1. First of all, paint the wooden board with whatever color you desire.

2. Let it dry for a day.

3. Click on the images tab on the left side of the panel and select an image from the huge library. If your desired image is unavailable, you can upload it.

4. After you have selected your image, they will appear in the canvas area.

5. Click on the **Edit** Toolbar to resize appropriately to fit your project

material. If you are using a rectangular piece of wood, make sure the size of the image is rectangular.

6. You can change the color of your image by clicking the **ColorSync Panel** in the upper layers panel on the left. Drag and drop the object into the layer of your desired color.

7. Select **Make It**. A screen will pop up with a preview of your image.

8. Since you are using iron-on vinyl, you must mirror it. We have discussed the importance of mirroring an image in this book. When you click **Mirror** in the sidebar, your image will flip backwards on the mat.

9. Click **Continue** and proceed to connect your computer to your Cricut Maker machine.

10. Select your iron-on material from the list of materials.

11. Flip your iron-on vinyl material back on your mat. Insert the mat into the Cricut machine and press the arrow button on it to hold your mat.

12. Press the **Go** button and your Cricut maker will cut out your project.

13. Press the arrow button again to release your mat.

14. Weed out excess material.

15. Iron the vinyl with an iron, EasyPress or a heat press.

Made in the USA
Coppell, TX
24 January 2021

48738439R00069